Make Today
Incredibly Beautiful

Fearfully and Wonderfully Me
Motivational Planning Journal Volume Five

RIA STORY

Make Today Incredibly Beautiful

WHAT OTHERS ARE SAYING ABOUT RIA AND HER BOOKS:

"I want to start by saying thank you...You made me want to try at life because you made me realize that you can make it anywhere you want, no matter where or what you are from. THANK YOU SO MUCH!" JONATHAN, HIGH SCHOOL STUDENT

"Ria's book (Beyond Bound and Broken) is full of hope and inspiration, and she shows us that despite experiencing horrific trauma as a young adult, that if we choose to, we can get past anything with the attitude that we bring to our life...Her book is full of wonderful quotes and wisdom."
MADELEINE BLACK, AUTHOR OF UNBROKEN

"I am using your material to empower myself and my female clients. Thanks for sharing your story and a wonderful journey of growth."
SUE QUIGLEY, LICENSED CLINICAL THERAPIST

"Very few 'victims' would be willing to share such a personal story. However, nothing about Ria is average. She chose to rise above her painful past and now positions it in a way to offer hope and healing to others who've been through unspeakable abuse. Ria's faith and marriage keep her grounded as she reveals the solid foundation which helps her stand as an overcomer. Read this story and find yourself and your own story strengthened."
KARY OBERBRUNNER, AUTHOR AND FOUNDER OF AUTHOR ACADEMY ELITE, ON *RIA'S STORY FROM ASHES TO BEAUTY*

"Thank you, Ria, for bringing our conference to a close. You were definitely an inspiration to all of us! Awesome Job!"
MELINDA, PRESIDENT AGS

"Beyond Bound and Broken is a deeply inspirational book; one that will stay with you for years to come. The lessons are deep, yet practical, and her advice leads to clear solutions. This is a profoundly hopeful book. We all face pain, difficulty, and doubt but with resilience, we can lead vital, flourishing lives. Ria's story although sometimes painfully difficult to read because of the trials she endured is a story of great courage and compassion both for herself as victim and for those who betrayed her. Forgiveness is a strong theme as is courage. I would highly recommend this book to anyone who is struggling to move forward after experiencing a great trial." AMAZON CUSTOMER

"...it was awesome! Ria has a real gift. I came away with so many helpful tools! Thank you, Ria."
STEFANIE, CONFERENCE ATTENDEE

"May God continue to bless your efforts. Your triumph is a great joy, and a gift to all that would hear or read it."
LOUIS O., HUMAN RIGHTS ADVOCATE

"What an inspiration you are to all of us especially the women audience. Your book is a clear example & step by step guide on how to become an effective leader. It is so easy to read and simple yet meaningful which is the beauty of this book."
K. POONWALA, CUSTOMER SUCCESS MANAGER, ON *LEADERSHIP GEMS FOR WOMEN*

"I was truly inspired by your presentation and the life lessons taught."
JENNIFER, CONFERENCE ATTENDEE

DEDICATION

Dear Reader,

In 2013, I made a decision to leave my career and pursue my calling. It wasn't an easy decision. I gave up the security of a regular paycheck and great benefits. I also resigned from the job I had worked very hard to get and had gone to college for 10 years to become qualified for. It was a great job in a great organization, and I considered myself successful, especially considering where I had started.

But, as Mark Twain said, "The two greatest days in life are the day you are born and the day you discover why." On August 14, 2013, I found my "why." With it came the realization I was more interested in making a difference than making a dollar.

In full transparency, it hasn't been easy.

There were some ramen-noodle-budget months. I went an entire year without a haircut. We sold our house, our cars, moved to an apartment, cashed in our retirement funds, trimmed all unnecessary expenses, and invested everything into ourselves and starting our speaking/training business. Mack and I have sacrificed much during our journey to be where we are today.

However, I would do it all again in a heartbeat. I would definitely do some things differently, better, or sooner, but I wouldn't hesitate to make the same decision again. Why? Why would someone give up a great career, good salary, good health insurance, and start their "career" completely over, losing $30,000 their first year in business, and giving up nearly everything in order to pursue speaking, writing books, and inspiring others? Why?

Today it was for you. In 2013, I had no idea I would be writing this dedication to you for this journal. But, I knew I wanted to make a bigger difference in the lives of others. Today, it's you.

"God will give you a double measure," someone once told me. "You don't understand, He already has." I replied.

It's true! Today, Mack and I are incredibly blessed, not only with material things but also by the rewards that come from the work we do. And so, this motivational planning journal is dedicated to YOU.

CONTENTS

1   A Note From Ria   ix

2   How To Make Today
    Incredibly Beautiful   xiv

3   Daily Motivational Planning
    Journal Pages   1

Make Today Incredibly Beautiful

A NOTE FROM RIA

Every one of us wants a life of meaning, achievement, and fulfillment. We all have hopes, dreams, and goals to become the best version of ourselves, and we all yearn to achieve our potential in life. The desire, or more accurately the *need*, to become the best version of ourselves is part of the human experience and the human story. Something inside you is shouting, "I want to reach my potential and become the person God created me to be."

We were created for a purpose. The greatest joy is realizing our purpose, and the greatest satisfaction is fulfilling it. We honor the gifts God gave us when we steward them well in answer to His calling.

Maslow's Hierarchy of Needs begins at the bottom with basic needs (food, water, and shelter) and progresses up the levels to the top (self-actualization). Only after each level of the hierarchy has been satisfied is it possible to move up. In other words, it's rather difficult, or perhaps impossible, to reach your God-given potential if you are scrambling each day to simply find food and a place to sleep. It's simply a matter of not being able to direct your energy toward fulfilling your calling if you are using that energy toward fulfilling the more basic needs.

Energy may never actually be lost, but time certainly is. And, *your* energy is finite just like your time on earth. Since you are reading this, you may not literally be scrambling to find food and shelter today. But figuratively, when we are unable to execute on the small daily disciplines, we are unable to fulfill the higher calling on our lives.

Consider the words of Hal Elrod, "Remember that who you're becoming is far more important than what you are doing, and yet it is what you're doing that is determining who you're becoming."

You can't "be all that you can be" until you master the basic discipline of daily choices. The greatest gap in the world is the gap between what we know we should do and what we do. How many times have you heard you should drink eight glasses of water every day and exercise at least three times a week? But, do you actually do it?

We don't fail to reach a goal because we are broken in some way, or there is something wrong with us. When a baby is born, we call it a miracle. We don't become any less miraculous as we age. We don't turn from miracle to mediocre by our 10th birthday. We aren't broken, just human.

We often have great intentions but lack the ability to execute. Something fun gets in the way, life happens, or unexpected problems get in the way of our priorities. And sometimes, we let inconsequential things get in the way of what we most need to do. Then, we get frustrated with ourselves, give up completely, and hope to do better tomorrow, next week, or next year.

And when that happens, we may never reach our goals or build our dreams.

We somehow fail to reach our God-given potential either because we don't believe it's possible or because we are unwilling to make the sacrifices necessary to turn our vision into our reality.

Let me assure you, it's possible. We are "Fearfully and Wonderfully Made" (Psalms 139:14), and God doesn't create mistakes, only miracles. I am "Fearfully and Wonderfully" me, just as you are "Fearfully and Wonderfully" you. God created each of us with potential. Transforming ourselves into the person who can reach our potential is up to us. Personal transformation is a process that occurs over time with consistent, intentional improvement and forward progress.

Let me also assure you: It's not going to happen by accident.

And, that's where the sacrifice comes in. We actually must do something different if we want life to be different. Vision alone isn't enough. We must take action.

Our lives are our stories, and we write a chapter every day by the actions we take and the choices we make. Each day we make the right choices, we build integrity by honoring the commitments we make to ourselves and to others and become more in alignment with who we were intended to be.

John C. Maxwell said it this way, "Every time we choose action over ease, we develop an increasing level of self-worth, self-respect, and self-confidence."

The key to reaching our potential is living life on purpose, with purpose, for a purpose. We must make every day matter. It's important to know what your priorities are, **but it's just as important to live them out each day.**

And when we do, we realize the power to make every day "incredibly beautiful" is within us.

When I realized living life on purpose was the key to reaching my potential, I became rather single-minded about it. I still am.

The power of focus and living out my priorities has enabled me to achieve amazing things. Not because I'm special, but because the principles of intentional living, applied discipline, and consistent execution are.

Trust me, there's a wide gap between being a trafficking victim and becoming a TEDx speaker, author, and certified leadership trainer.

I left home at 19 to escape my abusive father. He started sexually abusing me at age 12 and was trafficking me to men he met on the internet by the time I was 18. Learn more about how I overcame my childhood and teenage years in my book, *Bridges Out of the Past: A Survivor's Lessons on Resilience.*

When I left home, I didn't have a car, any money, or even a high school diploma. My first job was waiting tables in a pizza restaurant for $2.13 an hour. I was proud to have it. But, I didn't want to stay there the rest of my career. I'm not a genius, but I knew the job of my dreams wasn't going to come find me at Pizza Hut.

Using the principles I'm sharing with you in this planning journal, I moved beyond my past and began creating my future.

I earned three degrees, including an MBA with a cumulative 4.0 GPA. I got married and became a step-mom. I taught elite level group fitness classes to inspire others to be healthy physically. I competitively raced mountain bikes, winning four state championships in two years. I had a great career as the director of compliance with responsibilities for over 6,000 policies and millions of dollars in Medicare appeals for a large hospital. I ran seven marathons. (26.2 miles is a long way to drive, much less to run!) I shared the stage with Motivational Speakers Les Brown and John C. Maxwell. I spoke at TEDx Wilmington Women. I wrote many books on leadership and personal growth. I shared my story to help others learn how to overcome obstacles.

And, my story is still being written. Yours is too. We can achieve nearly anything when we are willing to do what it takes. It's not easy, but it is possible. And most importantly, it's worth it. Stop waiting for the right time, a better time, or more time. Most often, we are the ones who get in our own way, and overcoming most obstacles in life is easy compared to overcoming ourselves.

In the words of my husband Mack, "Make it happen or someone else will. It might as well be YOU."

If you want to get in touch, ask a question, or share a success story, E-mail me at: ria@riastory.com

HOW TO MAKE TODAY INCREDIBLY BEAUTIFUL

Incredibly Beautiful days are, well, incredibly beautiful. Maybe you've had the pleasure of having an "Incredibly Beautiful" day in the past. A day where you felt fully alive, full of hope, and you know you accomplished great strides in the direction of your dreams. A day where you got the most important things done with seemingly little effort. A day where you didn't forget something (or someone) important, had time to dream, hope, plan, and at the end of the day, you felt filled with positivity about how you spent your time and energy.

Whether you have experienced an Incredibly Beautiful day yet or not, they are possible. And, they begin with intentional thinking, resilience in the face of adversity, and hope and vision of the future. It seldom, if ever, happens by accident. But, when you start each day with a resilient mindset, you will achieve your priorities based on your values. Just a few minutes of intentional thought every morning will allow you to focus your energy, increase your influence, and make your day Incredibly Beautiful!

There are four dimensions to life: Physical, Mental, Spiritual, and Relational. Each dimension needs nurturing because if we fail to steward one dimension of life properly, we will become unbalanced. This leads to "failures" in one dimension, which ultimately causes failures in other dimensions.

Think of the busy executive who never has time to exercise. He may be very successful at work (one part of the social/relational dimension of life), but his lack of exercise leads to a heart attack (the physical dimension of life). And, recovering from the heart attack, he realizes his

xiv

marriage is crumbling because he is never home. Distracted by a difficult divorce, he loses focus on his job and misses a deadline for a client. One day he suddenly realizes his health is bad, his job is at risk, his marriage is over, and he experiences a spiritual crisis of faith. "Why me, Lord?" He asks, bitterly blaming God for the consequences of his choices.

Certainly, we don't cause all of our problems in life. Life is hard, bad things happen, and there will be challenges. But, we do create many of our problems just like we can create solutions to them.

Every day we make hundreds if not thousands of choices, some seemingly insignificant. Those choices, cumulatively, create our future. We make our choices, and then, our choices make us. We can choose our thoughts, mindset, attitude, values, and actions, but we cannot outrun the consequences of those choices, positive or negative.

This is simply how life works.

Good choices lead to increased influence with other people, improved circumstances, more options, more opportunities, and better results.

Poor choices lead to bad results.

Good choices begin with intentional thought, core values, and the discipline to stay true to them. You may not always get it right even when you try. But if you never try, you almost certainly won't get it right. As Hal Elrod said, "The degree to which you accept responsibility for everything in your life is precisely the degree of personal power you have to change or create anything in your life."

In his book, "The 7 Habits of Highly Effective People," Stephen R. Covey stated the first three habits of personal victory are: 1) Be Proactive, 2) Begin with the End in Mind, and 3) Put First Things First.

I like to think of these habits this way:

1) **Choices create freedom.**
   As a human being, I have the freedom to make choices. Though there is much I cannot control, regardless of what happens, I can *always* choose my response to what happens. Therefore, I am response-able which means I am responsible for the choices I make. The right choices create more freedom in the future.

2) **Vision inspires action.**
   As a human being, created by a divine God, I have a God-given purpose and gifts to fulfill that purpose. I'm "Fearfully and Wonderfully Me." Even if the vision isn't yet clear, I need to know the direction I want to go to get closer to the goal. Once I have a vision of where I'm going, it's much easier to be inspired in spite of distractions and take action in spite of obstacles.

3) **Execution requires discipline.**
   It's not enough to plan my priorities, I must execute based on my priorities. The secret here is setting small intentional goals to begin with in order to build integrity with myself. Much like my physical muscles get stronger with exercise, my mental discipline will also get stronger when exercised. Self-discipline means giving myself a command and following through with it *without making excuses*.

With big dreams and bigger goals, I quickly realized becoming highly effective wasn't going to happen by accident. I have juggled many hats over the years, including working multiple jobs, going to college, balancing family commitments, and trying to stay healthy, all at the same time.

I realized how much better my days, weeks, and months were when I lived them on purpose, with purpose, and for a purpose, so I started searching for a tool that would help me live with more intention and in alignment with the three principles above. I needed something that would help me with balance and to be more effective in every dimension of life.

I had in mind a planner or daily journal that was easy to use, simple to understand, and wouldn't take up too much time. I needed a place for reflections and a daily motivational thought or quote for personal growth (Mental dimension), a reminder to practice gratitude (Spiritual dimension), somewhere to list my healthy living plan for the day (Physical dimension), space to list my top priorities for the day in order to accomplish my goals and to increase my influence with others (Relational dimension).

I couldn't find one.

I've purchased many journals over the years. I've purchased various calendars, personal planners, wall calendars, desk organizers, daily timers, and I have five calendars on my iPhone, including two personal Google calendars, two for business, and one just to keep up with Mack. (Just for fun, I love to add things to his calendar!)

At some point, I gave up on finding exactly the right tool for me. I created a Word document on my computer with an outline that helped me set my top priorities for the day in each dimension of life.

That's how the idea for my "Motivational Planning Journal" series was born. I'm pretty sure I made the term up. But since what I was looking for apparently didn't exist, there wasn't a name for it either.

How do you use it? It's simple. Spend the first few minutes of your day with your Motivational Planning

Journal. Sit down and spend just a few minutes first thing every morning filling out two pages. Reflect and think about the quote. Then, complete each section. It's not complicated, but it is effective.

To become intentional, create an intentional habit. Our habits either serve us or enslave us. Trust me, this habit will serve you and serve you very well.

"I don't have time in the mornings," you may be thinking. Or, "I have too much to do."

A moment of truth: we make time for what's important to us. You might have to get up a little earlier, quit hitting the snooze button, or hide in the closet with a flashlight if all else fails.

Whatever it takes. A few minutes is not too much to commit to if you want to make your day resilient, incredible and beautiful.

Make the commitment to make the first few minutes of your day the most productive, and the rest of your day will take care of itself.

Once you capture your intentions in your planning journal, it will be much easier to follow through. Keep your planning journal with you. Throughout the day refer back to your priorities, commitments, and remember what you are grateful for.

When your take out order is wrong at the drive through, pull out your planning journal and remember you can choose your response. Remind yourself that the right response will increase your influence while the wrong one will decrease it.

When you are tempted by chocolate donuts at the office, pull out your planning journal and remember your commitment for being healthy today was to have an apple instead of a donut.

And, when you have an occasional slip-up, don't throw

in the towel. Pick yourself up, dust yourself off, and put away your excuses. Own it and then improve it.

Once the 60 days are complete, you may want to flip back to day one and see how far you've come. Celebrate your progress and then keep going.

There are several journals in the series. Each journal has different quotes and a different "theme" to appeal to different seasons of life.

Choose a theme of resilience if you are going through a tough time. Choose a theme of productivity if you are challenged with a big project in your life. Choose a theme of motivation if you are feeling a little down. (Find a complete list of journals at https://riastory.com/journals)

Using your planning journal every day will help you harness the power of affirmation and living on purpose. Doing this enables you to achieve more of what's truly important based on *your* priorities and values.

One last reminder: Saying "no" to less important things creates the space, time, and freedom to say "yes" to more important things. Now that you have identified your priorities and goals for the day, don't allow other things to derail you. It's easy to say "no" with a smile when you are saying "yes" to something bigger.

Here's to making today, and every day, Incredibly Beautiful.

Make Today Incredibly Beautiful

Daily Motivational Planning Journal Pages

"Adversity doesn't create your character - it reveals it."

~ Ria Story

Today I'm grateful for:

Reflections & Thoughts:

Leading Me Well - One thing I will do today to be physically healthier is to:

Make It Happen - Priorities Today:

1)

2)

3)

Influencing Others Well - I will intentionally add value or be kind to someone today by:

"We can't gain any momentum moving toward tomorrow if we are dragging the past behind us."

~ Jack Hayford

Today I'm grateful for:

Reflections & Thoughts:

Leading Me Well - One thing I will do today to be physically healthier is to:

Make It Happen - Priorities Today:

1)

2)

3)

Influencing Others Well - I will intentionally add value or be kind to someone today by:

"Character is developed daily, not in a day."

~ Mack Story

Today I'm grateful for:

Reflections & Thoughts:

Leading Me Well - One thing I will do today to be physically healthier is to:

Make It Happen - Priorities Today:

1)

2)

3)

Influencing Others Well - I will intentionally add value or be kind to someone today by:

"Extraordinary people survive under the most terrible circumstances and then become more extraordinary because of it."
~ Robertson Davies

Today I'm grateful for:

Reflections & Thoughts:

Leading Me Well - One thing I will do today to be physically healthier is to:

Make It Happen - Priorities Today:

1)

2)

3)

Influencing Others Well - I will intentionally add value or be kind to someone today by:

"Although it may be difficult to face the ugly pain of our past, we cannot conquer what we are not willing to confront."

~ Chawanis Ash

Today I'm grateful for:

Reflections & Thoughts:

Leading Me Well - One thing I will do today to be physically healthier is to:

Make It Happen - Priorities Today:

1)

2)

3)

Influencing Others Well - I will intentionally add value or be kind to someone today by:

"At the root of resilience is the willingness to take responsibility for results."

~ Eric Greitens

Today I'm grateful for:

Reflections & Thoughts:

Leading Me Well - One thing I will do today to be physically healthier is to:

Make It Happen - Priorities Today:

1)

2)

3)

Influencing Others Well - I will intentionally add value or be kind to someone today by:

"Character cannot be developed in ease and quiet. Only through experience of trial and suffering can the soul be strengthened, ambition inspired, and success achieved."

~ Helen Keller

Today I'm grateful for:

Reflections & Thoughts:

Leading Me Well - One thing I will do today to be physically healthier is to:

Make It Happen - Priorities Today:

1)

2)

3)

Influencing Others Well - I will intentionally add value or be kind to someone today by:

"Our destiny is not created by the shoes we wear...but by the steps we take."

~ Unknown

Today I'm grateful for:

Reflections & Thoughts:

Leading Me Well - One thing I will do today to be physically healthier is to:

Make It Happen - Priorities Today:

1)

2)

3)

Influencing Others Well - I will intentionally add value or be kind to someone today by:

"Every woman or man who got to where they are now started from where they once were."

~ Ria Story

Today I'm grateful for:

Reflections & Thoughts:

Leading Me Well - One thing I will do today to be physically healthier is to:

Make It Happen - Priorities Today:

1)

2)

3)

Influencing Others Well - I will intentionally add value or be kind to someone today by:

"Far from being a disadvantage, struggle is a decided advantage, because it develops those qualities which would forever lie dormant without it."

~ Napoleon Hill

Today I'm grateful for:

Reflections & Thoughts:

Leading Me Well - One thing I will do today to be physically healthier is to:

Make It Happen - Priorities Today:

1)

2)

3)

Influencing Others Well - I will intentionally add value or be kind to someone today by:

"Go for it now. The future is promised to no one."

~ Wayne Dyer

Today I'm grateful for:

Reflections & Thoughts:

Leading Me Well - One thing I will do today to be physically healthier is to:

Make It Happen - Priorities Today:

1)

2)

3)

Influencing Others Well - I will intentionally add value or be kind to someone today by:

"Don't let yesterday hold today hostage."

~ Ria Story

Today I'm grateful for:

Reflections & Thoughts:

Leading Me Well - One thing I will do today to be physically healthier is to:

Make It Happen - Priorities Today:

1)

2)

3)

Influencing Others Well - I will intentionally add value or be kind to someone today by:

"I am not what happened to me, I am what I choose to become."

~ Carl Jung

Today I'm grateful for:

Reflections & Thoughts:

Leading Me Well - One thing I will do today to be physically healthier is to:

Make It Happen - Priorities Today:

1)

2)

3)

Influencing Others Well - I will intentionally add value or be kind to someone today by:

"If the world thinks you're not good enough, it's a lie. Get a second opinion."

~ Nick Vujicic

Today I'm grateful for:

Reflections & Thoughts:

Leading Me Well - One thing I will do today to be physically healthier is to:

Make It Happen - Priorities Today:

1)

2)

3)

Influencing Others Well - I will intentionally add value or be kind to someone today by:

"It takes character to harness powerful and instinctive feelings and redirect our thoughts toward positive attitudes, but those who do live happier lives in a happier world."

~ Michael Josephson

Today I'm grateful for:

Reflections & Thoughts:

Leading Me Well - One thing I will do today to be physically healthier is to:

Make It Happen - Priorities Today:

1)

2)

3)

Influencing Others Well - I will intentionally add value or be kind to someone today by:

"It's not your story that defines you, it's what you do with your story that defines you."

~ Jason Vale

Today I'm grateful for:

Reflections & Thoughts:

Leading Me Well - One thing I will do today to be physically healthier is to:

Make It Happen - Priorities Today:

1)

2)

3)

Influencing Others Well - I will intentionally add value or be kind to someone today by:

"Learn from yesterday, live for today, hope for tomorrow."

~ Albert Einstein

Today I'm grateful for:

Reflections & Thoughts:

Leading Me Well - One thing I will do today to be physically healthier is to:

Make It Happen - Priorities Today:

1)

2)

3)

Influencing Others Well - I will intentionally add value or be kind to someone today by:

"Once you become fearless, life becomes limitless."

~ Unknown

Today I'm grateful for:

Reflections & Thoughts:

Leading Me Well - One thing I will do today to be physically healthier is to:

Make It Happen - Priorities Today:

1)

2)

3)

Influencing Others Well - I will intentionally add value or be kind to someone today by:

"Hope is being able to see there is light despite all of the darkness."

~ Desmond Tutu

Today I'm grateful for:

Reflections & Thoughts:

Leading Me Well - One thing I will do today to be physically healthier is to:

Make It Happen - Priorities Today:

1)

2)

3)

Influencing Others Well - I will intentionally add value or be kind to someone today by:

"Our greatest ministry comes from our deepest hurts."

~ Rick Warren

Today I'm grateful for:

Reflections & Thoughts:

Leading Me Well - One thing I will do today to be physically healthier is to:

Make It Happen - Priorities Today:

1)

2)

3)

Influencing Others Well - I will intentionally add value or be kind to someone today by:

"Our scars make us stronger."

~ Ria Story

Today I'm grateful for:

Reflections & Thoughts:

Leading Me Well - One thing I will do today to be physically healthier is to:

Make It Happen - Priorities Today:

1)

2)

3)

Influencing Others Well - I will intentionally add value or be kind to someone today by:

"Our sense of self is created and shaped by those around us. Once it's shattered, we must recreate it with help from others and hope for the future."

~ Ria Story

Today I'm grateful for:

Reflections & Thoughts:

Leading Me Well - One thing I will do today to be physically healthier is to:

Make It Happen - Priorities Today:

1)

2)

3)

Influencing Others Well - I will intentionally add value or be kind to someone today by:

"The world breaks everyone and afterward many are strong at the broken places."
~ Ernest Hemingway

Today I'm grateful for:

Reflections & Thoughts:

Leading Me Well - One thing I will do today to be physically healthier is to:

Make It Happen - Priorities Today:

1)

2)

3)

Influencing Others Well - I will intentionally add value or be kind to someone today by:

"They can conquer who believe they can."

~ Virgil

Today I'm grateful for:

Reflections & Thoughts:

Leading Me Well - One thing I will do today to be physically healthier is to:

Make It Happen - Priorities Today:

1)

2)

3)

Influencing Others Well - I will intentionally add value or be kind to someone today by:

"To develop yourself is to love yourself."

~ Kevin Hall

Today I'm grateful for:

Reflections & Thoughts:

Leading Me Well - One thing I will do today to be physically healthier is to:

Make It Happen - Priorities Today:

1)

2)

3)

Influencing Others Well - I will intentionally add value or be kind to someone today by:

"There are no hopeless situations, only people who have grown hopeless about them."

~ Andy Andrews

Today I'm grateful for:

Reflections & Thoughts:

Leading Me Well - One thing I will do today to be physically healthier is to:

Make It Happen - Priorities Today:

1)

2)

3)

Influencing Others Well - I will intentionally add value or be kind to someone today by:

"We aren't defined by our wins in life but rather by how we handle the losses."

~ Ria Story

Today I'm grateful for:

Reflections & Thoughts:

Leading Me Well - One thing I will do today to be physically healthier is to:

Make It Happen - Priorities Today:

1)

2)

3)

Influencing Others Well - I will intentionally add value or be kind to someone today by:

"What could have broken me made me."

~ Bob Chapman

Today I'm grateful for:

Reflections & Thoughts:

Leading Me Well - One thing I will do today to be physically healthier is to:

Make It Happen - Priorities Today:

1)

2)

3)

Influencing Others Well - I will intentionally add value or be kind to someone today by:

"What happens to us isn't as important as who we become because of it."

~ Ria Story

Today I'm grateful for:

Reflections & Thoughts:

Leading Me Well - One thing I will do today to be physically healthier is to:

Make It Happen - Priorities Today:

1)

2)

3)

Influencing Others Well - I will intentionally add value or be kind to someone today by:

"When you look back at the ruins of your past, remember rebuilding is the most important part of the story."

~ Ria Story

Today I'm grateful for:

Reflections & Thoughts:

Leading Me Well - One thing I will do today to be physically healthier is to:

Make It Happen - Priorities Today:

1)

2)

3)

Influencing Others Well - I will intentionally add value or be kind to someone today by:

"You cannot hang out with negative people and expect to live a positive life."

~ Darren Hardy

Today I'm grateful for:

Reflections & Thoughts:

Leading Me Well - One thing I will do today to be physically healthier is to:

Make It Happen - Priorities Today:

1)

2)

3)

Influencing Others Well - I will intentionally add value or be kind to someone today by:

"You should not be satisfied with being a victim, nor with being a survivor. You should aim to be a conqueror. There is an extraordinary quality of spirit that leads one to aspire to conquering rather than surviving."

~ Laura Schlessinger

Today I'm grateful for:

Reflections & Thoughts:

Leading Me Well - One thing I will do today to be physically healthier is to:

Make It Happen - Priorities Today:

1)

2)

3)

Influencing Others Well - I will intentionally add value or be kind to someone today by:

"Your best chance for success is reading. Learn to earn. Read to succeed."

~ Jeffrey Gitomer

Today I'm grateful for:

Reflections & Thoughts:

Leading Me Well - One thing I will do today to be physically healthier is to:

Make It Happen - Priorities Today:

1)

2)

3)

Influencing Others Well - I will intentionally add value or be kind to someone today by:

"Your history is not your destiny."
~ Alan Cohen

Today I'm grateful for:

Reflections & Thoughts:

Leading Me Well - One thing I will do today to be physically healthier is to:

Make It Happen - Priorities Today:

1)

2)

3)

Influencing Others Well - I will intentionally add value or be kind to someone today by:

"Choices always come with consequences. Choosing wisely brings the consequences we want in life."

~ Ria Story

Today I'm grateful for:

Reflections & Thoughts:

Leading Me Well - One thing I will do today to be physically healthier is to:

Make It Happen - Priorities Today:

1)

2)

3)

Influencing Others Well - I will intentionally add value or be kind to someone today by:

"We mistakenly believe that who we were is who we are, thus limiting our true potential in the present, based on the limitations of our past."

~ Hal Elrod

Today I'm grateful for:

Reflections & Thoughts:

Leading Me Well - One thing I will do today to be physically healthier is to:

Make It Happen - Priorities Today:

1)

2)

3)

Influencing Others Well - I will intentionally add value or be kind to someone today by:

"Don't let what you can't do stop you from doing what you can."

~ John Wooden

Today I'm grateful for:

Reflections & Thoughts:

Leading Me Well - One thing I will do today to be physically healthier is to:

Make It Happen - Priorities Today:

1)

2)

3)

Influencing Others Well - I will intentionally add value or be kind to someone today by:

"I can be changed by what happens to me, but I refuse to be reduced by it."

~ Maya Angelou

Today I'm grateful for:

Reflections & Thoughts:

Leading Me Well - One thing I will do today to be physically healthier is to:

Make It Happen - Priorities Today:

1)

2)

3)

Influencing Others Well - I will intentionally add value or be kind to someone today by:

"Owning our story can be hard but not nearly as difficult as spending our lives running from it."

~ Brené Brown

Today I'm grateful for:

Reflections & Thoughts:

Leading Me Well - One thing I will do today to be physically healthier is to:

Make It Happen - Priorities Today:

1)

2)

3)

Influencing Others Well - I will intentionally add value or be kind to someone today by:

"Life doesn't get easier or more forgiving; we get stronger and more resilient."

~ Steve Maraboli

Today I'm grateful for:

Reflections & Thoughts:

Leading Me Well - One thing I will do today to be physically healthier is to:

Make It Happen - Priorities Today:

1)

2)

3)

Influencing Others Well - I will intentionally add value or be kind to someone today by:

"Ninety-nine percent of failures come from people who have the habit of making excuses."

~ George Washington Carver

Today I'm grateful for:

Reflections & Thoughts:

Leading Me Well - One thing I will do today to be physically healthier is to:

Make It Happen - Priorities Today:

1)

2)

3)

Influencing Others Well - I will intentionally add value or be kind to someone today by:

"One of the most destructive limiting beliefs is the belief that I can justify unforgiveness."

~ Roger Nielsen

Today I'm grateful for:

Reflections & Thoughts:

Leading Me Well - One thing I will do today to be physically healthier is to:

Make It Happen - Priorities Today:

1)

2)

3)

Influencing Others Well - I will intentionally add value or be kind to someone today by:

"Our painful experiences aren't a liability, they're a gift. They give us perspective and meaning, an opportunity to find our unique purpose and our strength."

~ Edith Eger

Today I'm grateful for:

Reflections & Thoughts:

Leading Me Well - One thing I will do today to be physically healthier is to:

Make It Happen - Priorities Today:

1)

2)

3)

Influencing Others Well - I will intentionally add value or be kind to someone today by:

"Create the highest grandest vision possible for your life because you become what you believe."

~ Oprah Winfrey

Today I'm grateful for:

Reflections & Thoughts:

Leading Me Well - One thing I will do today to be physically healthier is to:

Make It Happen - Priorities Today:

1)

2)

3)

Influencing Others Well - I will intentionally add value or be kind to someone today by:

"The best remedy for those who are frightened, lonely, or unhappy is to go outside, somewhere they can be alone, alone with the sky, nature, and God. For then and only then can you feel that everything is as it should be and that God wants people to be happy amid nature's beauty and simplicity."

~ Anne Frank

Today I'm grateful for:

Reflections & Thoughts:

Leading Me Well - One thing I will do today to be physically healthier is to:

Make It Happen - Priorities Today:

1)

2)

3)

Influencing Others Well - I will intentionally add value or be kind to someone today by:

"The future belongs to those who believe in the beauty of their dreams."

~ Eleanor Roosevelt

Today I'm grateful for:

Reflections & Thoughts:

Leading Me Well - One thing I will do today to be physically healthier is to:

Make It Happen - Priorities Today:

1)

2)

3)

Influencing Others Well - I will intentionally add value or be kind to someone today by:

"The graveyard is the richest place on earth, because it is here that you will find all the hopes and dreams that were never fulfilled, the books that were never written, the songs that were never sung, the inventions that were never shared, the cures that were never discovered, all because someone was too afraid to take that first step."

~ Les Brown

Today I'm grateful for:

Reflections & Thoughts:

Leading Me Well - One thing I will do today to be physically healthier is to:

Make It Happen - Priorities Today:

1)

2)

3)

Influencing Others Well - I will intentionally add value or be kind to someone today by:

"There are no secrets to success. It is the result of preparation, hard work, and learning from failure."

~ Colin Powell

Today I'm grateful for:

Reflections & Thoughts:

Leading Me Well - One thing I will do today to be physically healthier is to:

Make It Happen - Priorities Today:

1)

2)

3)

Influencing Others Well - I will intentionally add value or be kind to someone today by:

"There are people out there that will never be helped unless they hear your story. They can only be helped by you. They need to hear you and no one else."

~ Les Brown

Today I'm grateful for:

Reflections & Thoughts:

Leading Me Well - One thing I will do today to be physically healthier is to:

Make It Happen - Priorities Today:

1)

2)

3)

Influencing Others Well - I will intentionally add value or be kind to someone today by:

"Time doesn't heal. It's what you do with the time. Healing is possible when we choose to take responsibility, when we choose to take risks, and finally, when we choose to release the wound, to let go of the past or the grief."

~ Edith Eger

Today I'm grateful for:

Reflections & Thoughts:

Leading Me Well - One thing I will do today to be physically healthier is to:

Make It Happen - Priorities Today:

1)

2)

3)

Influencing Others Well - I will intentionally add value or be kind to someone today by:

"We are products of our past, but we don't have to be prisoners of it."

~ Rick Warren

Today I'm grateful for:

Reflections & Thoughts:

Leading Me Well - One thing I will do today to be physically healthier is to:

Make It Happen - Priorities Today:

1)

2)

3)

Influencing Others Well - I will intentionally add value or be kind to someone today by:

"We may encounter many defeats but we must not be defeated."

~ Maya Angelou

Today I'm grateful for:

Reflections & Thoughts:

Leading Me Well - One thing I will do today to be physically healthier is to:

Make It Happen - Priorities Today:

1)

2)

3)

Influencing Others Well - I will intentionally add value or be kind to someone today by:

"If you can dream it, you can do it."

~ Walt Disney

Today I'm grateful for:

Reflections & Thoughts:

Leading Me Well - One thing I will do today to be physically healthier is to:

Make It Happen - Priorities Today:

1)

2)

3)

Influencing Others Well - I will intentionally add value or be kind to someone today by:

"We must accept finite disappointment, but never lose infinite hope."

~ Martin Luther King Jr.

Today I'm grateful for:

Reflections & Thoughts:

Leading Me Well - One thing I will do today to be physically healthier is to:

Make It Happen - Priorities Today:

1)

2)

3)

Influencing Others Well - I will intentionally add value or be kind to someone today by:

"Each one of us is more than the worst thing we've ever done."

~ Sheryl Sandberg

Today I'm grateful for:

Reflections & Thoughts:

Leading Me Well - One thing I will do today to be physically healthier is to:

Make It Happen - Priorities Today:

1)

2)

3)

Influencing Others Well - I will intentionally add value or be kind to someone today by:

"Forgiveness is unlocking the door to set someone free and realizing you were the prisoner."

~ Max Lucado

Today I'm grateful for:

Reflections & Thoughts:

Leading Me Well - One thing I will do today to be physically healthier is to:

Make It Happen - Priorities Today:

1)

2)

3)

Influencing Others Well - I will intentionally add value or be kind to someone today by:

"I learned that courage was not the absence of fear, but the triumph over it. The brave man is not he who does not feel afraid, but he who conquers that fear."

~ Nelson Mandela

Today I'm grateful for:

Reflections & Thoughts:

Leading Me Well - One thing I will do today to be physically healthier is to:

Make It Happen - Priorities Today:

1)

2)

3)

Influencing Others Well - I will intentionally add value or be kind to someone today by:

"There are people who've had it better than you and done worse. And, there are people who've had it worse than you and done better. The circumstances really have nothing to do with getting over your personal history. Past hurts can make you bitter or better—the choice is yours."

~ John C. Maxwell

Today I'm grateful for:

Reflections & Thoughts:

Leading Me Well - One thing I will do today to be physically healthier is to:

Make It Happen - Priorities Today:

1)

2)

3)

Influencing Others Well - I will intentionally add value or be kind to someone today by:

"You aren't a victim until you say you are. You aren't disabled until you say you are. You aren't a failure until you say you are. It's possible - until you say it isn't."

~ Ria Story

Today I'm grateful for:

Reflections & Thoughts:

Leading Me Well - One thing I will do today to be physically healthier is to:

Make It Happen - Priorities Today:

1)

2)

3)

Influencing Others Well - I will intentionally add value or be kind to someone today by:

"She was unstoppable, not because she did not have failures or doubts, but because she continued on despite them."

~ Beau Taplin

Today I'm grateful for:

Reflections & Thoughts:

Leading Me Well - One thing I will do today to be physically healthier is to:

Make It Happen - Priorities Today:

1)

2)

3)

Influencing Others Well - I will intentionally add value or be kind to someone today by:

Check out more journals like this at RiaStory.com!!

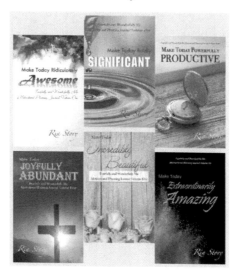

Make Today Ridiculously Awesome (Motivational)
Make Today Boldly Significant (Purpose)
Make Today Powerfully Productive (Execution/Action)
Make Today Joyfully Abundant (Faith Based – Joy/Gratitude)
Make Today Incredibly Beautiful (Resilience/Overcoming Adversity)
Make Today Extraordinarily Amazing (Making the most of today)

Excerpt from *PRIME Time: The Power of Effective Planning, by Ria Story*

I call it the *"whirlwind life."* You feel like you are living life in a tornado.

The vast majority of people in our society today are overcommitted, overstressed, overscheduled, too tired, and too busy. Most of them will tell you they don't like it.

Either, they don't know how to change it, or they aren't willing to. The former problem can be corrected by applying the principles in this book or by moving permanently to a deserted island where you are the sole inhabitant and completely cut off from all communication with the outside world.

The latter problem can only be corrected when the person *is* willing to change what needs to be changed.

Change isn't easy. It always requires more effort to make changes than it does to maintain the status quo. Changing your life is going to require energy, effort, self-discipline, and of course, time.

Work-life balance. It sounds good, like most lofty ideals do. But, how many of us have a good work-life balance? The term *"work-life balance"* assumes there is a life in there somewhere among all the work. However, for many of us, actually getting to the *"life"* part (or getting there with enough energy to enjoy it) is our biggest challenge. How often are you too exhausted by the end of the workweek to really enjoy Saturday morning spent with the kids because you are too busy catching up on laundry or working in the yard? There simply wasn't enough time to do your chores during the week. Or, you worked 10 plus hours per day at the office/job and still brought work home with you, so you could catch up.

Warning signs and symptoms that you may be experiencing the *"whirlwind life"* include: always running late or behind schedule, total exhaustion at the end of each and every day, forgetting commitments or appointments, and/or finding yourself unprepared for the day. Like the time I was 100% committed to going to the gym, but realized when I got there, I hadn't brought my sneakers.

The solution is simple. We need to manage time better, right?

Wrong. Nothing could be farther from the truth.
In reality, no one can manage time. We can't buy it. We can't save it. We can't get it back. However, we can waste it. We can spend it. Or, we can invest it.

There is an entire industry focused on *"Time Management."* Millions of dollars are spent every year on planners, calendars, time tracking apps, and time budgeting software. There are literally hundreds of books on how to manage your time better, how to track where your time goes, and how to do it more efficiently. We hear phrases that sound great: *"Work-life balance"* or *"Manage your time, manage your life."*

Sometimes on the surface, the warning signs and symptoms seem easy to fix.

Does it sound too good to be true? It's not. It can be done. But, I won't promise it will be easy. If we want different results, we must do things differently. Making some of the changes in this book will require you to think deeply about what you truly want, what you truly value, and what you are truly willing to do to get it. You must be willing to make decisions, sometimes difficult decisions.

It won't happen overnight, and you won't get it right all of the time. None of us do. But, there is hope. So, stop waiting for the right time or a better time. Stop waiting for next year or soccer season to end. Stop putting off the important things in your life in order to do the pressing things.

This book is not for everyone. There are some people who will simply wish for life to be better or different but aren't committed to change. If you are looking for a quick-fix or an instant cure, this book is not for you.

Each section in this book has valuable information and a supporting exercise. Read the chapter. Then, complete the exercise. It's tempting to rush through the exercises or skip them entirely. You will get as much out of this book as you put into it. If you rush through the sections in an effort to get done, you will get very little from this book. Life likely won't change, and you will have simply spent some of your precious time wishing for life to be different or better instead of taking action to make it different or better.

The choice is yours – and as much as I would like to, I can't do it for you. You are the one in control of your life. Or, if you aren't in control of your life, you are the only one who can gain control of your life.

It's your life.
It's time to stop going through the motions each day.
It's time to create the life you want.
It's time to stop trying to manage time.
It's time to start managing your life.
It's time to start leading yourself.

EXCERPT FROM *ACHIEVE: MAXIMIZE YOUR POTENTIAL WITH 7 KEYS TO SUCCESS AND SIGNIFICANCE,* by Ria Story

"Character is the ability to meet the demands of reality."

~ Henry Cloud

Integrity has four components: 1) Character; 2) Courage; 3) Commitment (to self); and 4) Congruency (with others).

Character is the foundational component because all the other components are built on top of character. In fact, integrity is determined by character. And, character is the determining success factor in life.

Your character and integrity determine how you will face life's challenges. Your response to success, failure, joy, pain, sickness, health, poverty, wealth, and the *"demands of reality"* will all be based upon your character.

Character is based upon intangible characteristics that will determine your success: attitude, work ethic, perseverance, resilience, discipline, courage, humility, and many more. Character is not based upon, or determined by, your education, background, race, ancestors, or experiences in life. Each and every day, you are writing your internal script by choosing your values. Then, your script (resulting character based upon the values you have internalized) will dictate your decisions and responses in any given situation.

Competency is your talent, natural gifts, skills, and abilities. Our character, not our competency, determines how far we will go and what we will ACHIEVE. Unfortunately, many people spend years developing their competency and little time developing their character and integrity.

In June 2013, I went to Guatemala on a mission trip. This wasn't a mission trip like you usually hear about where you take medical supplies and teach the Gospel. It was a mission trip to start the cultural transformation of Guatemala. This initiative had been years in the making because the President of Guatemala had asked John Maxwell for support in teaching the nation personal leadership principles.

While I was in Guatemala, our team trained various leaders; from Boy Scout troop leaders to top-level government officials. 150 coaches trained over 20,000 leaders in three days. One of the things we shared with them was 87% of who we are is determined by our character. The other 13% is what we know, our skills, knowledge and technical abilities. In other words, 87% of our success and influence comes from what we are, not what we know.

It's not always easy to live true to your values. Sometimes, having character requires you to face uncomfortable truths and stand up for what you believe. This happened to me early in my career.

I had recently been promoted to a new position in the organization where I worked. My new role was one of two identical positions in the organization. "Christy" (name changed) was my counterpart, and we had the same job duties and expectations. Christy had been there many years and had settled comfortably into her routine, so I knew I could learn from her.

I had a good work ethic, and I was eager to continue to make a good impression, hoping to continue moving up in the organization. Always a quick learner, I watched carefully how Christy did her job, and then I tried to see if I could make the process more efficient. I made some mistakes but quickly learned how to be more effective and efficient in my new role. And, I didn't mind working hard, taking initiative, and stepping up without being asked.

One day, my boss called me aside. *"Hey Ria,"* she said, *"Come here a moment."*

"Sure," I replied, *"What do you need?"*

"I've got a little problem," she chuckled, *"And, I need your help."* Always eager to help, I nodded for her to continue. *"Ok, sure."*

"Everyone has noticed how quick you are learning, and you are really doing an outstanding job."

"Thank you!" I smiled, excited she had noticed my efforts and hard work.

"But the problem is, you are making Christy look bad. She's been here a lot longer and you are causing some problems for her. There are some concerns about why she doesn't do as good a job as you are doing. And, people are asking me why I let her get away with slacking off."

I could feel my smile starting to melt. *"Oh?"*

"Can you just slow down sometimes and try not to be so fast at your work? I don't mean you have to screw up on purpose but maybe wait until someone asks you before you do something that needs to be done."

I couldn't believe it. My boss was telling me I needed to slack off because Christy didn't want to work hard.

I knew she and Christy were friends outside of work. They took trips together, went out for lunch, and even had drinks after work sometimes too. I also knew I wasn't going to slow down for one minute. I wasn't making Christy look bad, she was making me look good.

It put me in an uncomfortable position, but I told my boss I wasn't going to compromise my work ethic. And then, I showed her by continuing to work as hard as I could. Within two years, I had her job.

Character is having the right values. Integrity is living true to them. We must have the character to meet the demands of reality and the integrity to choose to do so.

ABOUT THE AUTHOR

Like many, Ria faced adversity in life. Ria was sexually abused by her father from age 12 - 19, forced to play the role of his wife, and even shared with other men. Desperate to escape, she left home at 19 without a job, a car, or even a high school diploma. Ria learned to be resilient, not only surviving, but thriving. She worked her way through college, earning her MBA with a cumulative 4.0 GPA, and had a successful career in the corporate world of administrative healthcare.

Ria's background includes more than 10 years in administrative healthcare with several years in leadership and management including working as the Director of Compliance for a large healthcare organization. Ria's responsibilities included oversight of thousands of organizational policies, organizational compliance with all State and Federal regulations, and responsibility for several million dollars in Medicare appeals.

Today, Ria is a motivational leadership speaker, TEDx Speaker, and author of 11 books, including Leadership Gems for Women, and 6 Motivational Planning Journals. Ria is a certified leadership speaker and trainer and was selected three times to speak on stage at International John Maxwell Certification Events. Motivational speaker Les Brown also invited Ria to share the stage with him in Los Angeles, CA.

Ria has a passion for health and wellness and is a certified group fitness instructor. She has completed several marathons and half-marathons and won both the Alabama and Georgia Women's State Mountain Biking Championships in 2011 and 2012.

Ria shares powerful leadership principles and tools of transformation from her journey to equip and empower women, helping them maximize their potential in life and leadership.

ABOUT MACK STORY

Mack began his career in manufacturing on the front lines of a machine shop. He grew himself into upper management and found his niche in lean manufacturing and along with it, developed his passion for leadership.

With more than 20 years working with and on the front lines, he brings a powerful blend of practical experience and leadership knowledge to his clients. Mack is a published author of several leadership development and personal growth books: Blue-Collar Leadership & Culture, Blue-Collar Leadership, Blue-Collar Leadership & Teamwork, Blue-Collar Leadership & Supervision, Blue-Collar Kaizen, Defining Influence, 10 Values of High Impact Leaders, MAXIMIZE Your Potential, MAXIMIZE Your Leadership Potential, Change Happens, Who's Buying You?, and 10 Foundational Elements of Intentional Transformation.

He understands that everything rises and falls on leadership.

For more detailed information on Mack, please visit TopStoryLeadership.com.

For information on Mack's unique Blue-Collar resources, please visit BlueCollarleadership.com

Order books online at Amazon or RiaStory.com

Ria's Story

From Ashes To Beauty

Ria Story

In *Beyond Bound and Broken*, Ria shares how she overcame the shame, fear, and doubt she developed after enduring years of extreme sexual abuse by her father. Forced to play the role of a wife and even shared with other men due to her father's perversions, Ria left home at 19 without a job, a car, or even a high-school diploma. This book also contains lessons on resilience and overcoming adversity that you can apply to your own life.

In *Ria's Story From Ashes To Beauty*, Ria tells her personal story of growing up as a victim of extreme sexual abuse from age 12 – 19, leaving home to escape, and her decision to tell her story

Order books online at Amazon or RiaStory.com

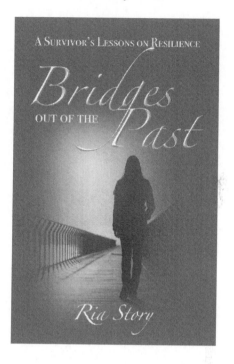

It's not what happens to you in life. It's who you become because of it. We all experience pain, grief, and loss in life. Resilience is the difference between *"I didn't die,"* and *"I learned to live again."* In this captivating book on resilience, Ria walks you through her own horrific story of more than seven years of sexual abuse by her father. She then shares how she learned not only to survive, but also to thrive in spite of her past. Learn how to overcome challenges, obstacles, and adversity in your own life by building a bridge out of the past and into the future.

(Watch 7 minutes of her story at RiaStory.com/TEDx)

Order books online at Amazon or RiaStory.com

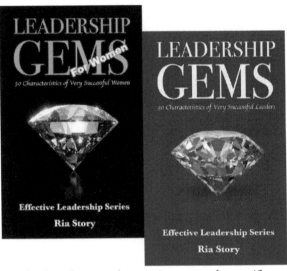

Note: Leadership Gems is the generic, non-gender specific, version of Leadership Gems for Women. The content is very similar.

Women are naturally high impact leaders because they are relationship oriented. However, it's a *"man's world"* out there and natural ability isn't enough to help you be successful as a leader. You must be intentional.

Ria packed these books with 30 leadership gems which very successful people internalize and apply. Ria has combined her years of experience in leadership roles of different organizations along with years of studying, teaching, training, and speaking on leadership to give you these 30, short and simple, yet powerful and profound, lessons to help you become very successful, regardless of whether you are in a formal leadership position or not.

Order books online at Amazon or RiaStory.com

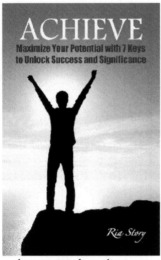

You have hopes, dreams, and goals you want to achieve. You have aspirations of leaving a legacy of significance. You have untapped potential waiting to be unleashed. But, unfortunately, how to maximize your potential isn't something addressed in job or skills training. And sadly, how to achieve success and find significance in life isn't something taught in school, college, or by most parents.

In *ACHIEVE: Maximize Your Potential with 7 Keys to Unlock Success and Significance*, Ria shares lessons to help you become more influential, more successful and maximize your potential in life. Three-page chapters are short, yet powerful, and provide principles on realizing your potential with actionable takeaways. These brief vignettes provide humorous, touching, or sad lessons straight from the heart that you can immediately apply to your own situation.

Order books online at Amazon or RiaStory.com

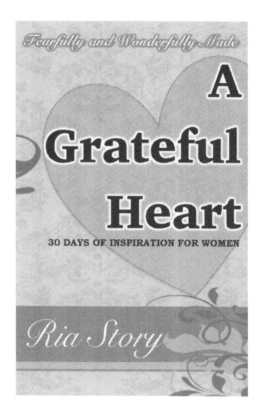

Become inspired by this 30-day collection of daily devotions for women, where you will find practical advice on intentionally living with a grateful heart, inspirational quotes, short journaling opportunities, and scripture from God's Word on practicing gratitude.

Order books online at Amazon or RiaStory.com

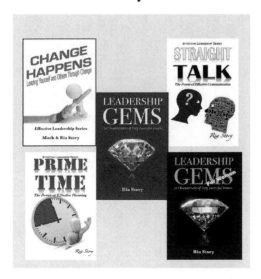

Ria's *Effective Leadership Series* books are written to develop and enhance your leadership skills, while also helping you increase your abilities in areas like communication and relationships, time management, planning and execution, leading and implementing change. Look for more books in the *Effective Leadership Series*:

- *Straight Talk: The Power of Effective Communication*

- *PRIME Time: The Power of Effective Planning*

- *Change Happens: Leading Yourself and Others through Change (Co-authored by Ria & Mack Story)*

- *Leadership Gems & Leadership Gems for Women*

Order books online at Amazon or
TopStoryLeadership.com

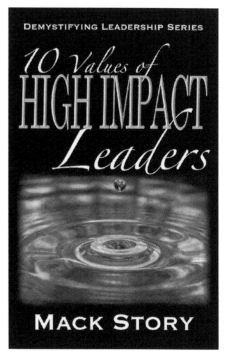

High impact leaders align their habits with key values in order to maximize their influence. High impact leaders intentionally grow and develop themselves in an effort to more effectively grow and develop others. These *10 Values* are commonly understood. However, they are not always commonly practiced. These *10 Values* will help you build trust and accelerate relationship building. Those mastering these *10 Values* will be able to lead with speed as they develop 360° of influence from wherever they are.

Order books online at Amazon or BlueCollarLeadership.com

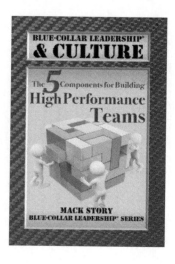

It's easier to compete when you're attracting great people instead of searching for good people.

Blue-Collar Leadership® & Culture will help you understand why culture is the key to becoming a sought after employer of choice within your industry and in your area of operation.

You'll also discover how to leverage the components of The Transformation Equation to create a culture that will support, attract, and retain high performance team members.

Blue-Collar Leadership® & Culture is intended to serve as a tool, a guide, and a transformational road map for leaders who want to create a high impact culture that will become their greatest competitive advantage.

Down load the first 5 chapters FREE at:
BlueCollarLeadership.com/download

Order books online at Amazon or BlueCollarLeadership.com

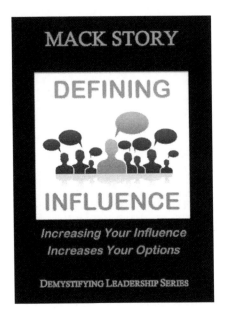

Are you looking for transformation in your life? Do you want better results? Do you want stronger relationships?

In *Defining Influence*, Mack breaks down many of the principles that will allow anyone at any level to methodically and intentionally increase their positive influence.

Mack blends his personal growth journey with lessons on the principles he learned along the way. He's not telling you what he learned after years of research, but rather what he learned from years of application and transformation. Everything rises and falls on influence.

Order books online at Amazon or BlueCollarLeadership.com

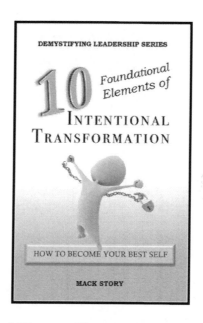

10 Foundational Elements of Intentional Transformation serves as a source of motivation and inspiration to help you climb your way to the next level and beyond as you learn to intentionally create a better future for yourself. The pages will ENCOURAGE, ENGAGE, and EMPOWER you as you become more focused and intentional about moving from where you are to where you want to be.

All of us are somewhere, but most of us want to be somewhere else. However, we don't always know how to get there. You will learn how to intentionally move forward as you learn to navigate the 10 foundational layers of transformation.

Order books online at Amazon or
TopStoryLeadership.com

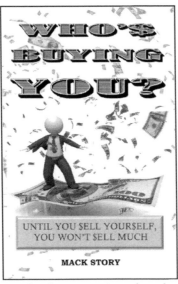

"Sales persuasion and influence, moving others, has changed more in the last 10 years than it has in the last 100 years. It has transitioned from buyer beware to seller beware" ~ *Daniel Pink*

So, it's no longer *"Buyer beware!"* It's *"Seller beware!"* Why? Today, the buyer has the advantage over the seller. Most often, they are holding it in their hand. It's a smart phone. They can learn everything about your product before they meet you. They can compare features and prices instantly. The major advantage you do still have is: YOU! IF they like you. IF they trust you. IF they feel you want to help them. This book is filled with 30 short chapters providing unique insights that will give you the advantage, not over the buyer, but over your competition: those who are selling what you're selling. It will help you sell yourself.

Order books online at Amazon or BlueCollarLeadership.com

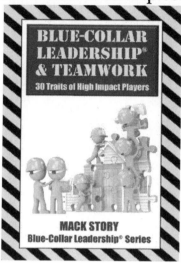

Are you ready to play at the next level and beyond?

In today's high stakes game of business, the players on the team are the competitive advantage for any organization. But, only if they are on the field instead of on the bench.

The competitive advantage for every individual is developing 360° of influence regardless of position, title, or rank.

Blue-Collar Leadership® & *Teamwork* provides a simple, yet powerful and unique, resource for individuals who want to increase their influence and make a high impact. It's also a resource and tool for leaders, teams, and organizations, who are ready to Engage the Front Line to Improve the Bottom Line.

Down load the first 5 chapters FREE at:
BlueCollarLeadership.com/download

Order books online at Amazon or BlueCollarLeadership.com

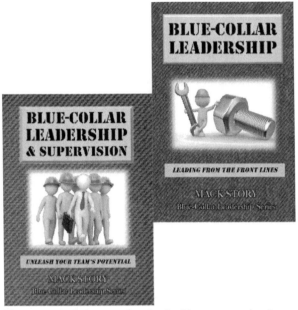

"I wish someone had given me these books 30 years ago when I started my career on the front lines. They would have changed my life then. They can change your life now." ~ Mack Story

Blue-Collar Leadership® & Supervision and *Blue-Collar Leadership®* are written specifically for those who lead the people on the frontlines and for those on the front lines. With 30 short, easy to read 3 page chapters, these books contain powerful, yet simple to understand leadership lessons.

Down load the first 5 chapters of each book FREE at: BlueCollarLeadership.com/download

Order books online at Amazon or BlueCollarLeadership.com

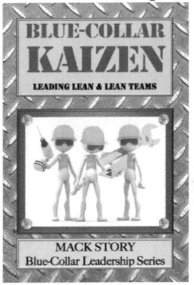

The biggest challenge in process improvement and cultural transformation isn't identifying the problems. It's execution: implementing and sustaining the solutions.

Blue-Collar Kaizen is a resource for anyone in any position who is, or will be, leading a team through process improvement and change. Learn to engage, empower, and encourage your team for long term buy-in and sustained gains.

Mack Story has over 11,000 hours experience leading hundreds of leaders and thousands of their cross-functional kaizen team members through process improvement, organizational change, and cultural transformation.

**Down load the first 5 chapters FREE at:
BlueCollarLeadership.com/download**

Order books online at Amazon or TopStoryLeadership.com

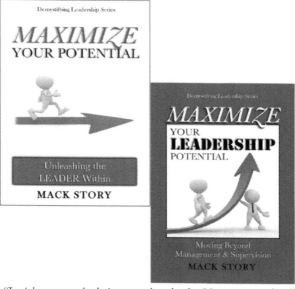

*"I wish someone had given me these books 30 years ago when I
started my career. They would have changed my life then.
They can change your life now." ~ Mack Story*

MAXIMIZE Your Potential will help you learn to lead yourself
well. *MAXIMIZE Your Leadership Potential* will help you learn to
lead others well. With 30 short, easy to read 3 page chapters,
these books contain simple and easy to understand, yet powerful
leadership lessons.

*Note: These two MAXIMIZE books are the white-collar, or non-specific,
version of the Blue-Collar Leadership® books and contain nearly identical
content.*

147